Star Seeds: Manual a

Starseeds Intro: Manual and Handbook

By: Sara Starfire

Thank you to my best friend, soul mate, and husband Sky for always supporting my endeavors. A wife couldn't ask for a better partner to have in all of her lives. Also thanks to all of my students, clients and random strangers who give me inspiration on a daily basis. This book couldn't have been written without you.

Introduction

This book is intended for all starseeds who have decided to incarnate on Earth. It wasn't an easy journey for most of us to embark upon, none-the-less, you are here and you do have a mission that you are to fulfill. When I first started my own personal experience, I was averse to accepting that I too, am a "Starseed". I went through many nights in self-doubt and wondered how it is that I could possibly fit in with those "weirdo's". I was in denial. While all at the same time, I fully believed in extraterrestrials and their connection to mankind and the human race. Yet, I never wanted to classify, or even thought it possible to be classified in a proverbial alien race.

Through my own experiences I have compiled a book to help you too, the Starseeds to find their origins, purpose in life, their relationship patterns and how to use those gifts to better mankind. This book is no way a means to say that everyone is "alien" and that we do not posses human DNA. I ask that you read the book with an open mind, yet be fully skeptical of the content provided. I do not ever try to understand to know how the universe works. I use my intuition, spirit guides, angels and other resources to pass on to you the information that you are about to read. I have lined out some of the chapters as an owners manual and other's as personal essays. As you read through this book, look for any subtle body reactions to something that you may read. If you find it repulsing, you may have found a past life block that could open up more answers for you. If you have a particular "A-Ha" moment, pay attention to that as well. As always, I highly recommend keeping a journal and writing all of your experiences down.

Star Seeds: Manual and Handbook

Chapters

The Awakening	7
The Origins of Mankind	16
Angels and Aliens	22
Who are Starseeds?	29
18 Ways To Know If You're A Starseed	35
Starseed Origins	39
Diet, Health and Nutrition	59
Reiki, Crystals, and Channeling	68
Working With Your Ultra-Sensitivity	74
Conclusion	88

The Awakening

There has been a planetary shift in the making since December 21, 2012. It was subtle at first; like babies waking up from a nap wiping their eyes. Slowly mankind has been on a sort of spiritual journey and identity crisis. As a professional counselor, I have seen the shift happen over the past three years. Within the last year, I have seen a major awakening that has begun to open up. More and more "humans" are starting to find that their soul origins may not be from this planet after all. They are beginning to see that their souls are limitless and can exist on other multidimensional levels and planes of existence. Through my past experience I have met these people from the angelic realms, elemental realms, ancient human realms, and also extraterrestrial realms. Upon meeting them, it's almost an instant recognition of meeting an angel, fairy, alchemist and a star seed. Yet, these categories are difficult for humans to understand because they are often lost in a cloud of fear, anxiety, self-doubt, and denial. For some, and the many that I have come to meet, a veil has been lifted from their eyes and they see the world as it is for the first time ever. Many times have I heard, "Is that why I can't fit in anywhere?" or "I just got chicken skin".

For some of us, it can literally rock us to our core and we go into denial until we had enough time to process the awakening.

My personal experience happened in March of 2014. I had taken Doreen Virtue's on-line class of Earth Angel Realms. I flew threw the course, absorbing everything that there was to learn, and immediately turned around and began to apply it in my counseling sessions and in classes. While I enjoyed the class and felt that Ms. Virtue had indeed tapped into something powerful, I felt frustrated that I couldn't find my realm. I skipped through realms that I thought maybe could fit me, but didn't quite stick. I tried the Mermaid realm, Atlantean, and fairy realm. While they each seemed to play some sort of role, I was still lost until one day someone on a forum, someone suggested that I was from the Starseed realm, and suggested that I go back and study that section again. I watched the video and read the book about Star Seeds three times. Each time I felt more and more attracted to it, but also a weird, "no, I don't want to be associated with those people. I want to be "normal". That's when it finally dawned on me that I was indeed a Starseed. There was no more denying it, and instead of feeling repulsed, I actually became excited. I knew that having that feeling of repulsion was a karmic past life connection to my soul's origin. If I could accept that I was indeed a star seed, then I could easily begin to connect with my life purpose and how I was going to help other people. At the time, I had just been contracted to counsel at Hawaii's premier metaphysical store. I needed to figure out who I was, so that I could properly channel information for other people.

Sometime after that awakening, I astral projected to a green planet. I was fully conscious during the dream and noticed a protective bubble surrounded me. I took my finger and moved it along the atmosphere and watched it change to a trail of liquid bubbles. Over my left should was a city in the distance. It was iridescent and had spires that looked like Hindu temples. Over my right shoulder was a very tall angel, maybe close to nine feet tall. He was a greenish purple color, and I couldn't see his face, but he wore a collared robe that hung down to his feet. He was my angel and he was alien in origin. When I asked him where we were he responded, "Andromeda". I said, "Oh, I'm home!" and immediately awoke. It was about four o'clock in the morning and I remember a lot of crying. It was so comfortable and beautiful; I felt immediate homesickness upon my return. I went to the couch and did a

Google search for Andromeda and found the personality traits for the star system.

In the following months preceding my awakening, I met several other people who were experiencing the same thing. I started working with them in private counseling sessions and began teaching classes. I started to notice though, that just like humans, there are several different races because no two personalities were alike. You can not just call a starseed, a starseed, and not have them want to learn where they came from. Many that I have met have never been to Earth before and seem to be a bit lost. They have a hard time fitting into the societal mold. They're usually techies, but some are more intellectual and some are more emotional. Some are natural channelers and some are natural healers. Some are both. Some have lived thousands of lives on other star systems, and that is why they may be drawn to more than one star cluster, and some may have lived on Earth for hundreds of lives. Some are more grounded than others; some are more adventurous than others. Some love animals and are vegans, some like animals and eat meat (though most star seeds eventually become vegan after their awakening). Each of them is here for a purpose though, and that is to help mankind reach a state of consciousness to raise the earth's vibration to take us all home.

Star Seeds: Manual and Handbook

The Origins of Mankind

In 1968 a revolutionary book emerged to the public; it was Eric Von Dänikens book "Chariots of the God's". For the first time, someone had started to theorize that perhaps man's origins aren't that complicated after all. Perhaps it's as simple as looking up to the stars. The book theorizes that the concept of man, and the origins of man can be traced back to Bible and connect us with ET origin. In Genesis 1:26 the Bible says, "And God said Let us make man in our image, after our likeness". The question simply is, who is "us, our"? Biblical theologians argue that this simply means the Father, Son, and Holy Ghost. However, this is before the holy trinity, and that of Jesus Christ. Also, why state it as a plural statement, yet have God say it? God since it's not plural makes one wonder if the "s" from "God" was dropped, and making the statement plural. It would have read instead, "And God's said, Let us make man in our image, after our likeness". When you add the "s" the statement makes a lot more sense. The book set on course a whirlwind of speculation and avid followers, and debunkers. Eric Von Däniken never sets out to destroy the bible. Instead, he believes that the bible is a link to our extraterrestrial origins and it's still applicable. He is a

Catholic and still believes in God. Yet biblical scholars, theologians, and debunkers (trolls) have tried and failed unsuccessfully to defame Däniken, yet his simple question has caught the attention of millions are readers from around the world.

There are several mentions in the bible that also speaks of angels and flying machines. Perhaps the angels that we know of today really don't look like humans with feathered wings, and blonde hair and blue eyes (and they don't), but are indeed aliens. I feel that the angels that set out to help in Sodom and Gomorrah; the angel who told Mary that she would be carrying the son of

God; and the angel who fought against Lucifer and cast him down to hell, where actually territorial fights to help ensure that humans stay on their paths.

And while Däniken brought a revolutionary question to modern man, it certainly wasn't the first time that our ancestor's had believed in these theories themselves. In fact from ancient Egypt, to the Mayan, Incan and Native Hopi Indians, there have been signs from the "Star People" that we were visited before. There are cave drawings in the Native American desert, the Nazca Lines in Peru, drawing's in pyramids and other area's of the world that distinctly show strange beings that oddly resemble extraterrestrial.

There are also ancient civilizations of the world that oddly match up with Orion's belt, like the Great Pyramids of Giza and the Mayan temples in Mexico at Teotihuacán, and the Sacred Alignment of the Hopi. Within all of these coincidences of manmade monuments, we have to ask, "Why did they build these monuments", and more importantly "Who told them to build these monuments". There is no possible way, even with the advent of human technology that we can replicate what the Egyptians created.

My objective is just to raise the question of possibilities. There is no sure fire answer to the history of mans origins; I simply believe that it is important to keep an open (but skeptical) mind on all areas that we theorize about. My personal belief is that the universe, God, and aliens have been working together since before Earth took its form. While that may seem delusional or even naïve to some, I feel that those who already believe that are generations a head of most human beings. When we understand these belief's we are ready to engage in the global consciousness shift, we understand that the human race should be working together and not against one another.

Angels and Aliens

We live in a world where angels are seen as long blonde curly haired beings, with expansive wings, and humanoid features. We can thank the church for that as they have over the centuries defined what we see and what we believe by their beliefs and standards. This isn't a new concept or idea, yet one that has been around since the dawning of the Catholic Church of the 11th century. In biblical text angels are mentioned from Genesis, to the birth of Christ, to Revelations. Angels play an important role in our connection with God because they are the messengers.

They communicate with us on a daily basis to help us through our own lives. They work closely with our spirit guides and make sure that we are fulfilling our missions and stay out of trouble (though some work hard than others obviously).

I believe that when we work with angels they will take on whatever forms that we are most comfortable with. In the past and still yet today, I feel that we are comfortable seeing them with humanoid features. I myself have seen my guardian angel in both an astral travel to my home planet and through past life regression. On both occasions he has appeared to me in alien form. In truth, angels have no body because they vibrate at such a high state of frequency. They take on their forms when they need to make themselves present to us. Most of the angels that I have seen with my naked eye are flashing orbs around people's shoulders, not in human form. Only on one occasion Archangel Michael made an appearance to me during a reading, even then only coming through my third eye area in full human form.

Whatever they look like, angels work with us on a multitude of levels depending on what it is that we need. There is a hierarchy of the angels that I feel holds true to the order of nature.

- Elemental kingdom: Fairies are the angels of nature and work closely with humans when gardening, cooking, and fae magic. You also find dragons, unicorns, mermaids and other "mythical" beings working in this realm.
- Angels: Those with the slowest frequency whose resonate is closest to humans are guardian angels. They work with the Archangels to ensure that you stay on your cosmic blueprint.
- Archangels: They responsible for the angels. The energy of the archangel is vast and they can send out millions of their angels,

who are aspect of their energy. You can ask for guidance from any Archangel and they will immediately be by your side.
- Principalities: They work closely with hospitals, large corporations and governments.
- Powers: They are better known as the Ascended Masters. Ascended Masters are humans and deieties who have lived on Earth before and ascended upon their death. Lord Krishna, Buddha and Jesus are some of the hundreds of Ascended Masters.
- The Virtues: They are responsible to ensure that change is happening on Earth and our

consciousness level is rising. Look to the sky and see beams of light coming through the clouds and you will see the Virtues.

- Dominions: They oversee the angelic order and make sure the angels are doing their jobs. They are here to ensure that our consciousness is rising.
- Thrones: They look after the planets; Lady Gaia, for example, is the throne in charge of Earth.
- Cherubim: Are angels of wisdom and are the guardians of the stars and the heavens. They spread unconditional love round the universe.

- Seraphim: They are God's right hand man. They are there to receive God's direct orders and make sure that they get channeled to the correct angels. Once the messages are passed on, the angels pass the messages onto the humans via the chain-of-command.

Who Are Starseeds?

They are volunteers who have incarnated here on earth to raise the vibration of mankind. They come from different galaxies, planets, and cosmos. Often times they are lost and confused on what their purpose here on earth really is. They feel homesickness, yet can't pinpoint to why that is. They often are attracted to science and spirituality, and look to the stars for answers. They are fascinated and yet terrified of the notion of aliens among us and will at times try to block any sort of memory associated with them. I have even found that many of them have been visited by their alien families and are being worked on or visited during their sleep. Many people associate this with terror, while others just feel a certain calm and peace about the entire experience. Depending on the level of awareness with the individual will determine how she/he will react to visitations.

This past year, I had a past life regression and visited my home planet in the star system Andromeda. I had been there once before during an astral travel, so I was excited to visit my home again. Upon meeting my angel (who was ET origin), we entered into a home that resembled a lot of a home on Star

Wars. It was dirt, but not dirty. As a matter of fact it felt very comfortable. There wasn't any furniture in the home, and the only resemblance of a home was what looked like a kitchen but I believe was used for healings. I was transformed into an infant and looked at my mother's face, which looked like... an alien. Except, with over accentuated lips almost like a caricature. We laughed and laughed and this went on for several minutes until my therapist finally brought us back around. The joy and sense of happiness that I felt was something I had never experienced before. It filled my heart with joy and wonderment and such love. Love that I have never experienced here on Earth before. Love that was so unconditional that I felt absolutely, undeniably, at home in my mother's arms.

Often times, people remark to me how much love that I am radiating, yet here on earth, I don't feel like I am. I feel like I have a heavy heart and that often times, it's hard to breath. I realize now that you, like me, probably are experiencing the harsh energy of the earth and the frequency that she carries. Often times, the hate and evil nature of some people becomes too much for us to bear. We seek solace in our homes and find ways to stay away from other people. This may continue for weeks or months, until yet again we are ready to head back out into the world and start our work all over again. It's okay to take breaks and to give yourself time to rest and recuperate. It's a myth that as a lightworker you have to work all of the time, and make a full time job at it. The truth is that your guides want what's best for you. If you are being nudged to slow down, do so. Don't feel fear or panic that rent won't get met, because it will. Taking a day or a week off of work will not break you. You can also still work, but cut back on how much that you are doing. Figure out what is important to you and stick with that. One of my wise friends from planet Sirius once told me to have something just for myself, and for me only.

Whether it's readings, writing, photography whatever; just make it mine and for me alone.

Once I realized this small truth everything else just started to fall into place. I realized that I don't have to save the world. I just need to help whomever I can, when I can. Whatever my calling, or yours, you don't need to kill yourself over it.

18 Way To Know If You're A Starseed

Here are some signs that you actually may be a Starseed:

1. A constant feeling of not fitting in. Being teased from an early age. Never quite feeling that you fit in even into adulthood.

2. A longing to fly, or do a lot of traveling. Having that feeling that you want to go home.

3. Changing your outward appearance. Changing hair color, style, style in clothing: I feel all of this is a way for us to try to figure out who we are.

4. Dreams or encounters with E.T.'s.

Feelings of encounters with extra terrestrials.

5. Love of Sci-Fi films and television shows. X-Files, Medium, Unsolved Mysteries anything having to do with the spiritual and unusual.

6. Actual love of science and spirituality as it is one. Believing that science and spirituality can coexist.

7. You abhor violence of any kind. Whether it's movies, television, world events, or personal events. If there is any indication of violence or confrontation, you are out of there.

8. You're a natural healer and channeler. You love to help people and animals and will go out of your way to do so. You're often working as a psychic, or healer.

9. Though you are helpful, and sweet, you also have a cool exterior. You are very guarded of who you let into your close circle.

10. Fascination with certain star systems or planets.

11. Social awkwardness. Putting your foot in your mouth.
Awkwardly feeling like the conversation is over, but not sure how to continue with your dialog.

12. You not only love to have the latest gadgets in technology, but also learn how to use them quite easily. You're a quick learner.

13. You have a fascination with ancient pyramids, temples, and ruins.

14. You are a bit aloof and

ungrounded. You tend to live your life daydreaming. It's hard for you to focus on mundane tasks.

15. You are a workaholic. Even on your days "off" you are still working.

16. You believe that angels are actually visitors from other worlds.

17. You have a strong sense of claircognizance. Or knowing. You know things before they happen, and you feel like information is continuously being channeled through to you.
18. You love to learn as much as you love to teach.

Starseed Origins

The following list provides star systems on which your soul may originate from. As you read through this list, look for hints and clues to whether you resonate with the attributes or not. You may find yourself fitting into several categories, which isn't surprising since all star systems are interconnected with one another, as is Terra (Earth). If you find yourself fitting into 85% of the list you may come from that star system or several of them. After reading the list, you should feel a sense of home or a draw to the star system. Take the next several weeks and meditate and ask your guides to help you decide if that is where your origins are from. Through meditation, and dreams you should find your confirmation quickly.

Just a quick word of warning: Don't get too hung up on where your Star

System origins come from. At the end of the day you are still a child of the Divine and you are of spirit. This list is only to provide you with a little more insight and not to overwhelm you with "what-ifs". If you find yourself constantly thinking about where you come from, it's best to step back and take a break. Only when you break will the truth be revealed. Forcing the answers will only block you leaving you feeling anxious, excited, and frustrated.

Andromeda

Key Personality Traits:

- Seeks freedom
- Inner drive to seek freedom
- Frequently changes jobs, homes, relationships
- Feelings of being trapped
- Lack of confidence/ self love
- Spiritual teachers and healers
- Enjoys travel
- Enjoys excitement, activity & variety
- Enjoys driving fast, or flying in planes
- Self-critical
- Can be needy
- Often discouraged by family for having psychic abilities
- Their mind is often lined with money and how they manage it. Unhappy = poor money management

Careers:

- Channelers
- Healers
- Animal psychics
- Psychics

- Counselors
- Psychologists
- Crisis therapists
- Social Workers

Relationships:

- May expect others to be critical of them
- Needs encouragement
- Needs to be believed in
- Needs positive confirmation
- May have bouts of sadness or depression

Apollonia

Key Personality Traits:

- Loves to learn
- Make strong psychics
- Have many talents and can learn quickly
- Questions deeply
- Many career interests and may change careers often
- Act like sponges
- Can learn many languages
- Do not allow themselves to be limited in any role
- They do not like being labeled
- Normally calm, can exude anger if they are labeled or backed into a corner
- Extremely self-sufficient, financially and emotionally
- Can be rather serious
- Goal oriented

Career:

- Psychics
- Energy healers
- Earth advocates
- Animal rights advocates
- Claircognizant abilities
- Counselors
- Therapists
- Engineering
- Technology
- Computers
- Science
- Teachers – especially with children

Relationships:

- Needs Freedom
- Separate checking accounts
- No restrictions
- Usually won't settle down, or will divorce once and never remarry.
- Extremely independent and will usually rule the roost.
- Need to be in dominant role

Arcturus

Key Personality Traits:

- Strong Personalities
- ADD/ ADHD tendencies
- Inner strength, fierce
- Fiery in nature
- Feeling of "mission" from childhood
- Constant searching until they discover their purpose
- Can be depressed or unhappy/ even restless if their purpose is not found
- Creative
- Good comedic timing
- Loves to travel, or dreams or traveling
- Very loving and kind hearts
- Gets bored easily
- Dramatic
- Energetic
- Does not like sitting still
- Mind is constantly moving
- Gets along better with animals than with people

Careers:

- Writers
- Artists
- Designers
- Public speakers
- Counselors
- Psychics
- Travel agents
- Ambassadors or diplomats
- Comedians
- Interior decorators
- Pet communicators
- Animal healers

Relationships:

- Not too many friends, tend to be loners because they are always on the go
- Hard to get close to
- Needs freedom
- Can feel trapped and will flee at the first sign of commitment
- Not comfortable sharing feels
- Easy to express anger

Maldeck

Key Personality Traits:

- Strong personalities
- Steady
- Determined
- Focused
- Asks many questions/ inquisitive
- Natural leaders
- Intelligent
- Technically minded
- Detailed oriented
- Analytical
- Observers of human nature
- Trivia experts
- Reserved, may appear distant, hard to approach

Careers:

- Managers
- CEO's/ CFO's
- Activists – political
- Engineers
- Science/ Math teachers
- Accountants/ Bookkeepers

- Alchemists
- Doctors/ Lawyers/ Psychologists

Relationships:

- Loving
- Honorable
- Loyal
- Trustworthy
- Straightforward
- Open when comfortable
- Needs to also receive these traits from others whether in a relationship, or friendship

Orion

Key Personality Traits:

- Strong personalities
- Connection to ancient Egypt
- Strong ideals and beliefs, will go to any length to uphold them
- Asks many questions/ very inquisitive
- Can be over analytical
- May scrutinize others and be judgmental
- More intellectual then feeling
- Demands respect
- Deep thirst for knowledge
- Natural skeptics
- Hard to accept new beliefs
- Critical of others and of themselves
- They are perfectionists
- Not many friends, but loyal for life to those who they become friends/ lovers with

Careers:

- Animal lovers
- Advocates for animals
- Animal psychics
- Philosophers
- Psychologists

- Teachers/ Administrators

Relationships:

- Intellectualizes emotions
- Must understand feelings, as opposed to just feeling
- Asks more questions to understand situations
- Uncomfortable with emotional situations
- Needs to understand that feeling is just as important as understanding

Pleiades

Key Personality Traits:

- Sensitive
- Loving
- Kind to a fault
- Wants to be happy
- Emotional
- The "angels" of the stars
- Sensitive to criticism
- Shy and quiet
- Passive aggressive
- Empathic – absorbs energy easily
- Enablers
- Co-dependent upon others
- Prone to escapism and false realities
- Dramatic
- Loves children and seniors
- Loves to snuggle

Careers:

- Natural healers
- Counseling
- Coaching
- Motivation coaches
- Teachers – especially with children

- Librarians
- Nurses, nursing homes and hospice
- Works well with seniors and children in any capacity
- Flight Attendants

Relationships:

- Faithful
- Trusting and trustworthy
- Needs lots of encouragement
- Wants to shine as sponsors, but shyness keeps them in the background
- Co-dependent
- May seem dramatic, but are misunderstood
- Needs to cry

Pvila

Key Personality Traits:

- Strong personality
- Strong psychic abilities
- Strong sense of pride
- Strong sense of humor
- Need to be the center of attention
- Love to party
- Practical jokers
- Very impulsive
- Can seem unapproachable at first
- Very caring
- Judgmental of strangers, but caring towards those they are close with.

Careers:

- Comedians
- Actors
- Actors
- Activists
- Performing Arts
- Psychics (though usually this is rare)

Relationships:

- Very loyal
- Devoted
- Can be overbearing at times
- Overlooks flaws in others
- Partner may feel neglected as Pvila's can be over involved in their own lives, and not meet the needs of others
- Needs freedom
- Needs privacy, which may be misinterpreted as being aloof from their partners

Sirius

Key Personality Traits:

- Focused
- Determined
- Stubborn
- Open to new ideas as long as it makes sense to them
- Strong beliefs, ideals and personal integrity
- Very private
- Doesn't share feelings easily
- They can scrutinize and be judgmental
- Future orientated
- Can be defensive
- May seem aloof, but they just aren't "here"
- Can be misdiagnosed with ADD/ ADHD as children
- Have many lives as American Indians, shamans, priestesses etc.
- Has a strong connection to Atlantis/ Lemuria

Career:

- Explorers
- Travel writers
- Healers
- Psychics
- Law enforcement
- Engineers
- Lawyers and Judges
- Military
- Correctional officers

Relationships:

- Loyal
- Trustworthy
- Expects the same from others
- Can lack communication
- May seem to be insensitive, but they are just internalizing their feelings
- Wants a serious relationship, but may have a hard time settling down due to their need of personal freedom and privacy

Vega

Key Personality Traits:

- Self-sufficient
- Independent
- Proud
- Strong willed
- Knowledgeable
- Trivia Collectors
- Creative
- Bore easily, needs constant activity mentally and physically
- Analytical
- Need to "feel" to understand on a deep level
- Responsible
- Nurturing
- Caring
- Cautious of sharing feelings

Career:

- Artists
- Designers
- Inventors
- Actors
- Architects

- Graphic designers/ artists
- Healers
- Works well with stones and crystals
- Health Care
- Teachers

Relationships:

- Need alone time
- Privacy is important
- Needs personal freedom
- Needs appreciation
- Often neglects personal needs to accommodate others first

Diet, Health and Nutrition

Because Starseeds are ultra-sensitive to their surroundings and to Earth's frequency, I often find that they have very sensitive systems. They are prone to developing IBS, anxiety, heart palpitations, Chron's disease, Celiac Disease, and food allergies or sensitivities. I certainly am no doctor and don't profess to know everything when it comes to medical issues. I do recommend that if you are experiencing any discomfort to go see a licensed physician to rule out anything serious.

The best thing that a starseed can do for themselves however it to take extra good care for themselves, that means eating right, exercising, watching the amount of intake of alcohol or cigarettes, and sugar. Because of our already sensitive system, we may choose to turn to drugs, alcohol or sugar to numb our senses and put our pain at ease. In doing so however, we open ourselves up to a state of hypersensitivity, and then we turn to medical doctors to numb our pain more with more drugs. It becomes a vicious and deadly cycle if not treated correctly.

I used to suffer from bronchitis and sinus infections every six months like clock work. As a child, my mom would do the motherly reasonable thing and take me to the doctor to get me medicine. As a result, my body started building up defense mechanisms against antibiotics until I was on the strongest stuff on the market. When I got into my teens, I started to notice digestive issues. Just thinking that they were normal, I never really spoke about it because I was embarrassed to talk about my stools. It's not a happy subject to talk to people about and is downright embarrassing at times.

After I became a vegetarian when I was twenty-years old, I noticed that my sinus infections were less and less, but I would still get congested after eating some cheese, or after drinking a beer. My digestive system continued to get worse and worse until I finally went to my naturopath. After a series of tests I found that I was allergic to wheat, gluten, dairy, soy, legumes and twenty-nine different foods. I was devastated. I had to go on a strict diet for three months to see how my body would react. I made it through my diet and in the process lost thirty pounds (which I really don't have that much to loose anyway). I also noticed that I was stronger, faster, and more athletic than before. I had a lot more energy and wasn't getting sick as much. I have, since my diet, been on antibiotics twice in the three years that I have been gluten free and vegan.

I believe that GMO's (genetically modified organisms) have played a major role in our food and our health. Many times over I have spoken to friends who are in their thirties and they have digestive issues, cancer, or benign tumors. I believe that switching to organic non-GMO is the best way to take care of you. However, for many Star Seeds, the damage is irreparable. We have lived so long with this chronic condition that even eating whole grain non-GMO foods can affect our digestive system.

Here are some ways that you can help yourself on a healthy new path for yourself. I don't expect everyone to fit all of this into your lifestyle at once, but do take one step at a time. If anything incorporate healthy eating and moderate exercise into your daily routine.

* Switch to a vegetarian, pescetarian, or vegan diet. Omit red meat completely from your diet.

* Omit or limit alcohol intake to one 8 oz glass of red wine per night.

*Get moderate exercise daily. Go for a brisk thirty-minute walk. That's all that you need to do. Anything beyond that is exceptional.

*Omit or cut out sugar – Nutella is a great substitute for chocolate bars.

* Cut down on salt intake. Your body needs salt and can't live without it. Just moderate how much salt that you take in, especially if you eat out a lot.
*Make sure that you meditate once a week and let yourself distress. If you need to schedule a massage, or a Reiki Healing.

*If you start to feel a cold come on, take the day off and stay home. Use that time to relax and switch to a juice diet for twenty-four hours. Get the vitamin C rolling through your blood stream. If that still doesn't help after a few days, schedule an appointment with your naturopath or MD.

*Rest, rest, rest. I'm guilty of this myself; however try to get in at least 7-9 hours of sleep per night. If you have insomnia try reading a book before bedtime and stay off of your cell phones as the screen produces serotonin which is the same as sunlight.

*Do not smoke. Even the vaporizers contain aluminum and other toxins that you are inhaling.

Reiki, Crystals, and Channeling

Because Starseeds connect with higher frequency vibrations, they are often well attuned to work with healing modalities such as Reiki and other healing practices. Starseeds find themselves drawn to healing humans, animals and even plants. Working with your angels and guides will assist you in learning how to work with your innate gifts. All Starseeds can do Reiki as it comes from the Pleiades system. It is an alien form of healing as are the other healing modalities. Essentially, when you work with Reiki, you are channeling spirit to work through you. You are only the vessel and really aren't doing anything. Because of this you really don't need to become a "reiki master" because you already are a master. You just need to learn the sign and colors to help you guide you through your clients, but your guides are the ones telling you what to do. You don't even realize that you're doing it! Have you ever been around someone when you were feeling down or depressed and walked away feeling happy and joyous? It's because that person that you were talking with gave you a healing. The best part is that the person who you were talking to didn't even know that they were giving you a healing which leaves them even more open and receptive to spirit.

I believe that it's important to learn how to work with your choice of healing modality, but as a Starseed you will be tapping into things much higher than Reiki. You will be channeling healings that are coming from high form angels and ascended beings. You can learn all that you want and spend all of the money that you have, but you will not just be using Reiki alone but a combination of healing technique's that haven't even been discovered yet. Incorporating crystals into your practice will only enhance your healings.

Each crystal holds a certain vibration to it and you, as a Starseed, can feel the energy off of each one, pinpointing without reference to their healing qualities. Some people get caught up with the notion that every stone has a significant meaning. I do agree with part of that. I also feel that each crystal can hold a separate healing modality based on the intention. Let's say for example that you are drawn to obsidian. Obsidian is known as a protector against negativity; however, you feel that it can also be used to aid in healing of a broken heart. Since the obsidian is a protector, then yes, it can aid in healing a broken heart, not only because of the properties but because you also believe that it will do so. It's about setting the intention. Once intention is set you can create and build whatever you want.

Starseeds are very powerful because they often have pure hearts. They can create and manifest anything that they want as long as it serves the higher good and not themselves. Once it becomes about their ego's then it becomes clear that spirit stops working through them, or lower level entities will start to channel them.

Starseeds also make excellent psychics and councilors and teachers. Again, because they are so open and are naturals at being claircognizant, they can easily channel (or talk) to higher realms. Of course, depending on that Starseeds own awakening process and what their own frequencies are, will determine what they can and can not connect with.

However you decide to work with spirit is up to you Starseed. You will change your path and your specialties many times throughout your life; the important thing is just to get started.

Working With Your Ultra-Sensitivity

Because Starseeds are not from this planet, they often have a difficult time grounding themselves. Grounding means being connected to the Earth and feeling in their body. Most Starseeds find it difficult to concentrate on the most mundane tasks because they are often daydreaming or channeling information. Often times, our guides are downloading information directly to us throughout the day. You can actually feel a cord in your neck or a tingly feeling around your crown chakra. That's your guides and they are speaking to you, even if you can't hear them.

We also find that because of our grounding struggles, that we are also ultra-sensitive. I have found that they are more sensitive than other humans because we have specific missions that we are trying to accomplish before we transcend. As a Starseed child, if your parents didn't understand your sensitivity, you may have been told that you are "too sensitive", or to "toughen up". The problem with these negative reinforcements is that we take it to heart because we want to please humans and will do whatever it takes to make them happy. Unfortunately, most Starseeds that I have met begin to believe this way of thinking because they trust everyone.

And why shouldn't they? After all, humans are all good right? This type of negative behavior can begin to become a truth to Starseeds and they begin to take things too personally for all of the wrong reasons.

Devon works at a retail store. Because of his Starseed origins, he's a hard yet friendly worker. He takes his job very seriously and can seem to have a bout of OCD (obsessive compulsive disorder) when it comes to having a clean and tidy department. He prides himself that he has the largest, yet tidiest of the departments in the store.

One morning, Devon goes into work to find a few items out of place. Nothing too big, but just a few items out of place and want to make sure that they have some proper training for the new people who are on board. He gets on the walkie and asks his manager who closed the night before, and while the manager responds positively, another co-worker gets defensive because she feels the remark is made directly at her and the company for being messy and not closing properly. Devon is devastated because he doesn't want to hurt anyone. He musters up the courage to work things out with his co-worker only to have her yell at him and make a scene. Because of his sensitivity, Devon shuts down and blames himself for his actions. 'He should have not said anything, he should be more careful, he should run away and live in the mountains in a cave where he will never hurt another person so long as he lives.'

The hard truth for any Starseed to understand is that Devon did nothing wrong. He could have approached the situation a bit different, but his actions were pure and to help teach the new employee, not to get anyone in trouble. Being ultra-sensitive can be a bother for a Starseed because no matter how "grounded" that they are, they feel like they just don't understand human behavior. I like to think of Data from Star Trek: New Generation. Data was an AI (artificial intelligence) that worked on the Enterprise. Because he was a robot he lacked human emotions, but because of his intelligence he wanted to understand human behavior and how they feel. For most Starseeds, we are the Data's of the world (though some may be more extreme than others).

Before you leave the house in the morning remind yourself that you are indeed a Starseed in a human body. When you start to feel like you're being bullied, or threatened in any way, put up your galactic shield and ask for protection. Call in Archangel Michael to assist you, and to give you strength, courage and protection.

Because how Starseeds think and feel (highly intelligent and highly sensitive) sometimes it's better to walk away from a situation before it escalates. This is difficult for a lot of people because we want to smooth things over with the other person. Sometimes giving that person space to breath and cool down is better than to aggravate a situation by insisting that you work things out. In time, they will come around and you may even find yourselves friends with them (if you choose to do so).

Remember, Starseeds are wonderful. They are friendly, intelligent, sweet and a lot of fun to be around, and because you are a natural healer you'll probably notice a lot of people that gravitate themselves towards you. Just be aware that not everyone has good intentions and that they may not be acting for the betterment of mankind. They may just be in it for themselves. If you find that's the case, don't be afraid to distance yourself and give that other person space. You don't have to be friends with everyone, or have everyone's approval, Starseed. Just yourself.

If there's one thing that your guides want you to know is that being ultra-sensitive is a gift and not a burden. Don't let others try to tell you otherwise. If this goes back to your childhood, you have a lot of deprogramming to work on. Learn how to work with your gift instead of against it.

Autistic children are ultra-sensitive and they see the world in a very different manner than the humans around them. I feel as Starseeds we have a lot in common with them and a lot that we can learn from them.

Samantha was working one day in Customer Service at an auto shop. A mother and her little boy came in and she could sense immediately that the mother was distressed and so was the little boy. When she approached them, the boy, about tens years of age, was squirming and crying and pulling and tugging his mother. The mother in the mean time was explaining to Samantha that she needed to get her fender replaced. Out of no-where a light touch was felt on Samantha's heart chakra. She at first was a bit taken back when she noticed that the little boy had reached up to touch her. The mom interjected and said that her son had autism, and then continued her story. Samantha looked at the little boy and telepathically tried to communicate with him letting him know that it's alright and she see's him, all while leaning with one hand on the counter speaking to his mother. Again, another light touch. This time, the little boy had taken

Samantha's hand and let it sit for just a moment. Samantha responded by grabbing his hand to hold it, and it initially scared the little boy. Then a few minutes later he said "bye", which in itself was a miracle because he never spoke.

The experience shifted something inside of Samantha who now realized that on top of being ultra-sensitive she understood that she could telepathically communicate with autistic children. She had had thoughts about it in the past, but could never really test her theory before. With autism we find that children may not be able to communicate like "normal" humans, but that's because they aren't normal. They are special and deserve to be treated as such. This isn't meant that they "are meant to be held back" from growth of any kind, but encouraged and loved to help them grow and fulfill their own spiritual journey. They are Starseeds and if other Starseeds can work with them, then a great good is at hand to help heal and work with everyone.

Here's a quick list on how you can shield yourself from the harsh sensitivities of Earth and the humans here:

*Call in Archangel Michael for protection

*Don't take everyone or everything personally. A lot of times it's a reflection of the others insecurities that they are projecting onto you.

*Moldivite, tektite, sugalite and other stones are good for Starseeds to use as protection, and surprisingly as a grounding stone since we come from the stars.

*Imagine a shield around your body before you leave the house. This is blue in color, and just for effect, let's adds in some cosmos stars and nebulas. Imagine that this is your shield for the day and nothing or anyone can penetrate it. Check it half way through the day, if it's running a little light, put some more color in it.

*Say some daily affirmations.

*Remember to forgive yourself even if you're not ready to forgive the other person yet. In time, you will heal.

*Most importantly is for you to remember that you are loved. You have unconditional love from source and the Divine, no matter what your circumstances. You may be a Starseed, but you are in human form this lifetime.

Conclusion

This short little book is one that I hope that you can take with you on the go and one that I hope you can reference over and over again. There are no limitations on what you can and cannot do in this life of yours. You volunteered to come here for a reason and I hope that you can find out your life purpose. Remember that everyone's life purpose is different and one isn't more important than another. It's just as important to be a good mother or father, than it is to be a teacher of teachers, or a well-known psychic. Each of us is all on our own path of discovery and this is just the start for you, and me.

I'm excited to see how the world will progress and how we will manage to ascend to the New Earth when the timing is right. In the meantime, thank you Star Seeds for joining us on this planet and I am honored that you are here helping us ascend to higher consciousness.

Made in the USA
San Bernardino, CA
15 January 2016